Passion Of The Heart

POEMS AND SHORT STORIES

By

William Garrett Wooodard

Copyright © 2006 by William G. Woodard

Passion of the Heart
by William G. Woodard

Printed in the United States of America

ISBN 1-60034-005-9

All rights reserved solely by the author. The author guarantees all contents are original and do not infringe upon the legal rights of any other person or work. No part of this book may be reproduced in any form without the permission of the author. The views expressed in this book are not necessarily those of the publisher.

Unless otherwise indicated, Bible quotations are taken from the New King James Bible and the New International Version of the Computer Bible.

www.xulonpress.com

Poetry Of The Heart

"For God so loved the world that He gave His only begotten Son, that whoever believes in Him should not perish but have everlasting life." John 3: 16 (NKJV)

"Trust in the Lord with all your heart, and lean not on your own understanding; "Proverbs 3:5(NKJV)

TABLE OF CONTENTS

An Author's Note
POEMS
Poetry of the Heart:
Seeker I Be (Matthew 7:7-12)
Not Just A Book A Promise (Matthew 6:32, 33)
A Never Ending Circle (1Corinithians 13:1-13)
Keeper Of the Hear (1Samuel 16:7)
Watchman/Messenger (Malachi 3:1-7)
Time Is Essential (Ecclesiastes 3:1)
A Prayer From the Hear t (Psalm 46)
Simply true is the Treasure (Revelation1:17, 18)
A Race of Endurance (Philippians 3:13, 14)
A Grandmother's Love (1Corthinians 13:13)
A Mystery So Sweet (Psalm 1)
An Age Old Mystery (Psalm 62)
Mindful of the Beyond (Matthew 6:34)
WONDERS OF A NEW DAY (Hebrews 11:1, 2)
REACH OUT THY HAND (Palm 46: 1)
RIDING THE TRAIN OF FAITH, HOPE, AND LOVE

Signature of the heart:
HOMEWARD I LOOK AT A WONDER (Genesis 1: 1-6)
TOGETHER FOREVER (Genesis 2: 24, 25)
UPON A MOMENT IN TIME (Proverbs 31: 10-31)
A PRAYER UTTERED IN THE WIND (Ecclesiastes 5:2, 3)
TO SEEK WITHIN (Proverbs 16: 9)
TWINKLE, TWINKLE (Genesis 1:16)
JOURNEY OF LIFE (Song of Solomon 4:10-15)

FAITH IS WONDERFUL (2Corinthians 5: 7)
HOPE HAS NO LIMITS (Mark 16: 19, 20)
A SOUL TOMENTED BY LOVE (1 Corinthians 7: 1-8)
PRAYER OF SINCERITY (1 Peter 5: 6. 7)
I WANT BUT UNABLE TO HAVE (1 Corinthians 6:18-20)
A VEXED MAN (1 Corinthians10: 13)
QUESTION OF THE HEART (Matthew 5: 31, 32)
OUIET REFLECTIONS (Psalm 62)
TURNING OF TIME (Matthew 6:34)
POTTER'S HAND (Jeremiah 18 1-11)
A MOMENT TO PAUSE (Psalm 138: 7, 8)
REFLECTIONS OF THE HEART (Psalm 123)
A GENTLE TOUCH (Psalm 23)
A WONDER CALLED RAIN (Psalm 121)
SIMPLE DOES IT (Ecclesiastes 3:15)
SIMPLE THEME OF THE LORD'S TOUCH (Psalm 1)
AND THE DARKNESS COMES (Psalm 142)
A BLESSED MORNING TO BE
A GUARDIAN ANGEL STEADY AND TRUE
A BLESSED MORNING
SHE HAD BROWN EYES OF PASSION
THE FOLLY OF WORDS SAID IN ANGER

Miracles of the Heart
SHORT STORIES
PAST THE PAIN TO THE GRACE OF THE LORD
(Fictional short story)
A Comet's Story of Faith, Hope, and Love (fiction)
The Battle at Sunset

ABOUT THE AUTHOR
A Journey of the Heart Continues On: A True Miracle Story
(nonfiction)
ECCLESESAISTES 3: 1-22 (NIV)
PSALM 62:1-12 (NIV)
A NOTE OF THANKS
BIBLIOGRAPHY

TO WHOM IT MAY CONCERN:
An Author's Note

The poetry I, William Garrett Woodard, write is inspired first from the Lord, Jesus Christ, in faith, hope, and love. Secondly, poetry is often times inspired by family, friends, and people I meet on a daily basis as each new day begins a new. There are no sexual insinuations in my poetry or stories I write. It does poetry little good to the reader who think the worst before reading the poem. Most of times we authors fail to reveal the beauty of a poem to the reader, or the reader fails to see the true meaning in a poem due to the readers own perspective on life. I am sorry for the readers who are unable to see the beauty all around them, and the goodness within one's own heart. A poem should paint a beautiful picture that touches the heart and soul of the reader reading the poem. In faith, hope, and love I write a positive outlook on life instead of a negative outlook on life. To bring the peace and joy the Lord brings into my life as the Lord reveals His blessings, miracles, and mysteries to me on a daily basis. The poems I write in this book have been written and completed with new titles so my journey of life may be read in another time and place.

Yours Sincerely in Christ

God Bless You,

William G. Woodard

A SEEKER I BE

He seeks to and fro,
A treasure so simple it be,
But hardly found by the humans eye,
A seeker of the heart he seeks,
He seeks faith that is steady and true,
He seeks hope that is dependable and strong,
He seeks love that is honest and sincere,
A book he opens;
Page upon page he reads,
Stories and images vividly clear,
A promise deep and dear revealed;
Upon reading the pages,
A promise made at the cross,
A sacrifice made out of love for all,
A beginning not an ending,
The seeker of Jesus Christ he be,
A treasure revealed a simple beauty,
And glory to all who seek with open eyes, mind, heart, and soul
Jesus Christ is the answer you seek;

NOT JUST A BOOK A PROMISE

A page I turn;
Upon reading my Father's book,
Gentle soft leather I hold,
A book called the Holy Bible,
My Father's word I read;
Words spill forward upon reading,
Words written for me to write in my heart;
Words of faith, hope, and love
Tenderness is revealed before my eyes
A promise through the stable,
A promise revealed on a cross,
A promise revealed in an open tomb,
Jesus is the promise revealed,
A bridge to all who has faith;
A bridge to cross in times of need;
A bridge to wash away our sins;
Jesus Christ the grace revealed,

A NEVER ENDING CIRCLE

Love endures all;
Love never seeks it own;
Love sees all,
Love never fails,
Love is patient,
Love is kind,
Love is trusting,
Love is faithful,
Love is hopeful,
Love is generous,
Love is caring,
Love is Jesus that knows all;
Keeper of the heart,

KEEPER OF THE HEART

The words are strong within;
Within my heat is a treasure;
A treasure of love,
A treasure of hope,
A treasure of faith,
Dig deep within my heart;
For you will see not me,
But Jesus written within my heart,

WATCHMAN MESSENGER

He knows what is right,
He knows what is wrong,
For he knows the heart of people;
He seeks the heart within,
Not what is on the outside?
He is reserved,
He is quiet,
Seeks the well being of others;
He is mindful of problems,
He seeks the solutions,
He is dependent on the Lord;
He is organized,
Not independent of the Lord;
He knows the Bible,
He knows what the Lord has made right;
He knows what is true,
He knows what is pure,
A problem solver,
A thinker,
Knows about time;
Knows his place,
A messenger is one who exhibits faith, hope, and love in Jesus.

TIME IS ESSENTIAL

God has a purpose and plan for you;
A chapter ends another begins with God,
For we trust in the Lord,
We seek not the past,
We seek not the future,
For the future takes care of itself;
Seek the here and now,
The present and opportunities before you;
That the Lord has put before you to see on a daily basis.
Open your eyes,
Open your heart,
To see the miracles of the day,
To see the Lord's blessings on a daily basis;

A PRAYER FROM THE HEART

I wish I may,
I wish I might,
Wish upon this star tonight,
Star a glow twinkling bright and strong,
Among the Lord's grand creation,
A wish not for man's power and prestige;
But wish for faith, hope, and love
A wish of the heart and of the soul;
I wish this night,
A prayer so simple,
But an impossibility by my own eyes;
A possibility by the Lord's eyes,
That the Lord sends a woman of heart;
A woman of faith and hope,
A woman of love and honesty,
May this void I feel be filled?
With the Lord's beauty,
A woman to add to my life;
A blessing indeed she be,
So I can show her the miracles I have seen;
So I can show her the blessings the Lord has revealed to me;
Upon the journey we call life,
Amen.

SIMPLY TRUE IS THE TREASURE

A treasure I found indeed;
Within one's heart,
A simple acceptance of the heart,
A simple belief of the heart,
A simple commitment of the heart,
Jesus steady and true,
Dependable to the end;
A friend indeed to all;
A friend in faith, hope, and love

A RACE OF ENDURANCE

A moment in time I saw her;
A moment in joy and peace,
A moment lost in time,
For a single moment my race ended;
Upon staring into her eyes,
I felt peace and joy,
I felt an enduring love,
I felt an enduring faith,
I felt an enduring hope,
Encompasses my soul and my heart;
But upon the wings of an angel she soared;
Long hair blowing in the wind of the angel's wings;
I stared in awe as she flew heavenward;
For I was never to see her again,
But to continue the race of endurance,

A GRANDMOTHER'S LOVE

Once upon time I did see,
Beyond the clouds of white,
Beyond the sky of blue,
Upon hearing the whisper in the wind;
I looked heavenward to see,
A sight dear to my heart,
I saw my grandmother at heaven's gate;
She whispered to me words of encouragement for daily living.
She told me to be faithful,
She told me to hope and dream,
She told me to love all things,
For gone she was in a moment in time;
But the words were written upon my heart;
Words of faith, hope, and love.
(This poem is dedicated to my Grandmother Woodard who died June 2005 of cancer)

A MYSTERY SO SWEET

A dream so sweet I saw once;
Upon the wings of angel I did see,
A sight that vexed my soul and my heart,
A faith deep and dear I saw,
A hope within flutters to the surface,
A love striking my heart,
A mystery to me was this emotion;
But only for a moment I felt alive,
For upon the wings of an angel she flew;
A mystery in faith, hope, and love
Written forever upon my heart,
As I continue on the journey called life;

AN AGE OLD MYSTERY

A vexation of the heart it is;
What it is that vexes me?
A simple word written upon my heart;
It be love that vexes me,
For I saw from a far she be,
She be with long hair,
Eyes that be full of life,
A rhythmic beating it be,
As my heart skips a beat;
Takes one look upon thee,
To know a man loves a woman;
For a bond of love they create no one can see,
For a bond of faith they create no one can see,
For a bond of love they create no one can see
The bond of faith, hope, and love
For that is the mystery that vexes me;
To thee how can this be?
For no one knows,
It is the age old mystery to me.

MINDFUL OF THE BEYOND

A ghost writer I seek;
A ghost of faith,
Beyond man's concrete veil;
A ghost of love,
A whisper the ghost be,
A ghost that is tossed to and fro;
For the ghost writes upon my heart;
Words of courage and strength,
Words of faith and hope,
Words of love and understanding,
For the Lord knows all and sees all;
For the Lord is the ghost writer of our lives. Amen

WONDERS OF A NEW DAY

Wings of an angel I do ride,
Upon this early morning,
I ride upon my angel's wings;
A breeze blowing in my face,
A guardian, indeed, to me;
A comforter in faith,
A comforter in hope,
A comforter in love,
A new chapter begins on this early morning,
A day full of the unknown,
A day full of wonder,
A day full of mystery,
A day full of miracles and blessings;
As I rise to the early morning sunrise,
Warmth encompasses me as the day begins,
I thank You, Lord, for the peace and joy and for my guardian angel
each day I walk...

REACH OUT THY HAND

Tale my hand;
Take it in faith,
Blind it maybe even though; it is steady,
Take it in hope so all dreams my be revealed,
Take it in love for gentle and true it is;
Two hearts find one another,
A man and a woman fall in love,
Their heart beat quickens upon eye contact,
As two become one whole heart;
A leap in faith steady and sure,
A leap in hope everlasting it be,
A leap in love sincere and gentle,
Ever watchful is the Lord,
As He sends His guardian angels,
To watch over the two hearts,
(Dedicated to my big brother, his wife, and family)

RIDING THE TRAIN OF FAITH, HOPE, AND LOVE

I ride in this train;
I think upon this ticket I hold in my hand,
A ticket bought in blood by God's only Son;
Jesus bought me on the cross,
A price He alone could pay,
A sacrifice only He could make,
A death only He could overcome,
A ticket given in faith;
A ticket given in hope;
A ticket given in love;
I received it willingly, the ticket
For I ride the train of faith, hope, and love
Jesus says,
"Leave your burdens at the door,
For all who come aboard may rest in assurance;
Of My grace to all who receive Me and admit;
Me into their hearts, I will always be there;
For you until the end of time,"
Upon hearing these, warmth encompasses;
Me as I ride the train in to tomorrow,
For only Jesus knows what will be on a daily basis in our lives.

Signature Of The Heart

"No temptation has overtaken you except such as is
common to man, but God is faithful who will not
allow you to be tempted beyond what you are able,
but with the temptation will also make the way of escape,
that you may be able to bear it." 1 Corinthians 10: 13 (NKJV)

**BUT HE SAID, "THE THINGS WHIICH ARE IMPOSSIBLE
WITH MEN ARE POSSIBLE WITH GOD."
LUKE19:27 (NKJV)**

HOMEWARD I LOOK AT A WONDER

Upon a blue sky, once
I look to ponder a sight I did see;
A wonder of majestic proportions,
Beyond what man sees
A veil I did see,
Beyond the skies and clouds;
A glorious sight to me,
How did I see?
A glorious sight to me;
One full of faith,
One full of hope,
One full of love,
Thank you, Lord
For allowing me to see beyond man's wall;
To seek the Lord out on a daily basis;
Amen

TOGETHER FOREVER

Upon twilight I stared in awe,
A sight I did see,
Two stars twinkling bright and strong;
A male star steady and true,
A female star sincere and true,
A mergence of two stars I witnessed,
A mergence of faith,
A mergence of hope,
A mergence of love,
In a blink of an eye;
I saw two become one star,
One star shining forth bright and true;
Oh, my, to witness a glorious sight,
Sent from heaven above;
I thank thee, my Lord

(Dedicate this poem to my mom and dad who have been married for 38 yrs. and still go strong)

UPON A MOMENT IN TIME

A sight I witnessed in time;
For it took a moment in time,
Time mixed with faith,
Time mixed with hope,
Time mixed with love,
A woman big in heart she was;
Carried away by the angels of heaven,
A glimpse of happiness to last an eternity;
I thank you, Lord
For giving me each chance;
To see the Lord's creation called woman;

A PRAYER UTTERED IN THE WIND

Words spill forth as I speak,
Words of hurts and deep with despair,
Words mixed with faith, hope, and love
Words uttered in agony of the soul,
Words uttered in desperation;
Shallowness engulfs the prayer,
For in anger I spoke to the Lord,
I wonder now whether the Lord;
Will be able to speak to me,
For a moment words,
Are scattered to the wind,
The Lord hears all words,
In grace the Lord sees all;
Within one's heart the Lord knows all;
Before I ask the Lord forgives,
And tells me to start fresh each new day,
Thank you, Lord
For listening to my complaints and praises;
Amen.

TO SEEK WITHIN

Once, in deep thought
I imagined a heart;
A heart beating steady and true,
For the spoke to me,
"Seek within the heart,
Seek a faith deep and strong,
Seek a hope deep and sincere,
Seek a love deep with meekness,
Seek past the hurts of the past,
Seek beyond what you are able to see;
Seek the Lord and you will see thee,
Beauty within all hearts,"
Thank you, Lord!

TWINKLE, TWINKLE

Up in the sky,
I see a shining bright object;
A star I do see,
Upon looking, I wondered aloud,
"Twinkling little star,
You so bright I wish,
To know your secret,
You shine so bright and strong,"
A whisper in the wind I do hear,
"In faith I twinkle bright,
In hope I twinkle with a firm foundation,
In love I believe in the unknown,
Put these three together to see;
The Lord's creation before you."

JOURNEY OF LIFE

Upon this journey called life;
I often wonder of the beauty before me;
For time is a maker of wonders,
I ponder the simplicity of a union made special,
A union between man and woman made by God,
In which we call marriage;
Oh how simple one's faith can be,
Oh how simple one's hope is to be,
Oh how simple one's love is steady and true,
Upon the mergence of two hearts to be one;
Oh blessed is this simple miracle of the Lord's grand creation.

FAITH IS WONDERFUL

Faith is trust in the Lord,
Faith is a blessing from the Lord;
Faith is a miracle of the Lord,
Faith is a simple belief,
A belief of the unseen,
Seek deep and you shall see.
How one word is unfathomable in meaning?
For to seek its meaning is to go beyond man's eyes;
To seek with the Lord's eyes,
Is to see faith has no limits,
A simple acceptance by me;
And wonders are revealed in the word called faith,

HOPE HAS NO LIMITS

A simple dream my hopes be,
For life is a race of doubts and fears;
My hope knows no limits to me,
For the Lord knows only possibilities,
For in hope we have dreams revealed;
In hope we have love without end,
In hope we know of faith,
In hope a simple trust revealed,
For the Lord reveals His blessings;
And miracles to us through our hopes and dreams;
Thank you, Lord!

A SOUL TORMENTED BY LOVE

Vexed is my soul, O' Lord
How can a beauty such as she be?
So attractive she be,
A beauty within her shines forth,
A beauty deep with a faith simply be,
A beauty defined by hopes that are simply to be,
A beauty shining forth love that warms my heart;
But she is so far away, Lord?
How can she be, Lord?
Is this love I feel or something else?
How can a man and a woman be?
In love with one another,
Yet not be able to be together;
Beyond these four walls,
Vex, I am Lord?
Am I forever to be alone?
I know this is selfish of me;
But I need to know Lord,

PRAYER OF SINCERITY

Warmth encompasses my heart and my soul;
Upon uttering a prayer of sincerity,
For I speak openly and honestly,
Laying my sins before the Lord;
Admitting my burdens and my wrongs,
Admitting I need help on a daily basis,
I need to seek forgiveness;
For the wrongs committed by me,
I need to open my eyes,
To the Lord's will,
I need to open my heart,
To the Lord' will,
I need to let the Lord's will be done in my life.
And at the end of the prayer;
I hear a whisper in the wind,
"Child of mine your sins have been forgiven,"
Speaks the Lord,
"Only by freely admitting to me;
In an honest way you have done,
I hear your prayer and needs,
Warmth encompasses me of the gentle reminder,
Of the Lord's love for all who seek Him,

I WANT BUT UNABLE TO HAVE

I want her, Lord
My deepest desire is to be with her, Lord
Yet, I know deep down within my heart
This is selfish desire of the flesh,
That burns within me, O' Lord
It is not a desire given in faith, hope, and love
But of a self-centered desire of the flesh,
Please Lord, release me of this feeling
Lord, forgive me
Lord, for I have sinned against You
Teach me Lord to seek Your Wisdom,
Teach me Lord to seek the faith on a daily basis,
Teach me Lord to seek the hope You have given me,
Teach me Lord to seek the love that knows no limits;
Lord, teach me to be accountable daily
Lord, teach me to have a forgiving heart
Lord, teach me to be responsible of my actions
Lord, I thank thee for listening
Even though, my words are of a selfish nature
A vexed Christian man

A VEXED MAN

My heart warms within me,
Upon looking at a friend I know,
For she is a beautiful creation of the Lord;
Long flowing hair of black
Blue eyes sparkling of life
But deep within I know I am wrong,
For I cannot have her, Lord
A sinful desire churns within me;
A connection made upon eye contact,
A faith encompasses two hearts,
A hope circles two hearts,
A love warms the two hearts,
For out of a selfish desire swells within me;
Yet, it is not to be for the Lord was not with me,
I look but cannot have,
I want but cannot love,
A bitter man I am,
For she is gone in a blink of an eye
Forgive me Lord of writing these selfish words. Amen.

QUESTION OF THE HEART

A prayer sweet and true;
Honest and sincere are the words,
Spoken in humility,
Vexed is my soul, O Lord
How can this be?
For it was not to be,
But it is to be,
A woman I think of upon uttering these words;
A woman small in stature I think of;
With blue eyes deep with love,
Black hair flowing softly in the breeze,
A fluttering in my heart begins on thinking of her;
Can this be, Lord?
Is this really to be, Lord?
Can love be so simply given without material possessions?
Can faith be so simple upon a bond between a man and a woman?
Can a bond in faith, hope, and love be forged without?
The simple touch of hands between a man and a woman;
My heart raises these questions, but to gently;
Remind me that this is the Lord's plan and creation.
I am to trust in the Lord in all things,
Upon answering the questions that vexes me so;

QUIET REFELECTIONS

At days end, I sit and ponder the day's events.
As blue as my mood may be;
Upon this time, warmth encompasses me.
A gentle touch of faith reveals all,
A gentle touch of hope fills my cup,
A gentle touch of love opens my eyes and my heart;
To the Lord's blessings and miracles to me;
Oh, how wonderful it is to see the Lord;
Through the fears and doubts of the day,
Thank You, Lord, for being there for me;
Amen

TURNING OF TIME

Upon a moment in time,
A simple reflection I take;
For upon this roller coaster of life,
Many things have happened to me;
Which causes fear and doubting in our lives?
But upon these thoughts warmth encompasses my heart;
A wave of faith, hope, and love fills me,
As I see the Lord's miracle at work in me,
The Lord took a piece of clay,
and molded it into something wonderful
The Lord took me and made me into this;
Miracle of what possibilities are,
When dreams and hopes are revealed,
For the Lord takes what seems impossible to me;
And makes it into possibilities in Jesus,

POTTER'S HAND

At the age of six, the Potter's hand took hold of me
The Potter molded me into something wonderful, indeed
For the Potter made a master piece in me;
With hope dreams were given to me,
With love a negative became a positive,
With faith the breathe of survival comes into me;
For in faith, hope, and love the Potter molded a miracle out of me.
For at the age of 33, I am still amazed
At the miracle the Potter made out of me;
A simple moment in time is all it takes,
For me to say, "Thank you to the Potter."
For the Potter brought me from death's door
To reveal to others His simple miracles,
And blessings on the Potter's grand creation called earth
Thank you for all you have done for me,
And keep doing for me as You, Lord, reveal Your
Miracles, blessings and mysteries to me;
I wake to each day Thank You, Lord!

A MOMENT TO PAUSE

At the age of 33,
I am amazed at what life brings to us;
I reflect upon a decision I freely made,
A decision to ask Jesus into my heart,
A commitment made out of love;
Though I may stray Jesus is always welcomes me home;
A protector in faith to be there for me,
I awed by the miracles Jesus made in me;
Though doubts and fears attack me on a daily basis;
Jesus gives me hopes of survival on a daily basis,
One page of my book of life is finished,
Another page is written by Jesus' hands,
Thank thee for the miracle You made in me,
Thank thee for the blessings revealed through me,
Thank thee for giving me the faith, hope, and love
To seek You, Lord, beyond my fears and my doubts.
Amen

REFLECTION OF THE HEART

A living miracle the Lord made in me;
A broken vessel full of cracks,
The Potter took hold of the broken vessel;
He mended me and molded me, the broken vessel
He added faith in the mold,
He added hope in the mold,
He added love in the mold,
The Lord made something new out of something old;
The Lord breathed life into me,
A will made out of faith, hope, and love
A will to survive,
A will to be disciplined in love;
A will molded to seek beyond the hurts and pains,
A survivor I be,
In me a heart that knows no limits,
Amen

A GENTLE TOUCH

Gentle is gentle be,
Gentle do gentle does,
Gentle splash of rain;
Gentle streaks of lighting,
Gentle clash of thunder,
Glow yellow to gray;
White is the wind clouds,
Gentle is the Master's Touch,
A painting of nature's fury,
A gentle reminder of the power;
The power of creation, the unseen
A gentle orchestra of the Master's hands,
A gentle touch of the Lord's will and His orchestra of angels;

A WONDER CALLED RAIN

A gentle wonder I saw,
Upon a moment in time,
A majestic sight I did see;
Streaks of white come before my eyes,
Clash of cymbals as the orchestra starts up,
A cloud burst I see,
As rain flows forth,
An orchestra led by the Lord,
As angels play the instruments,
Instruments of faith, hope, and love

SIMPLE DOES IT

Simply be is the theme,
Simply is time;
Simple is a moment in time,
Simple is life,
Just look,
At the scene before you;
A sight for all to see;
A hope given by the Lord,
A love not with standing,
A faith knows no bounds,
A sunrise a gentle reminder,
For all, how precious is time to thee,

SIMPLE THEME OF THE LORD'S TOUCH

Simple is the theme of life;
Simple as the touch of the Lord be;
A simple faith given of love,
A simple hope to fill one's heart,
A simple love given out of a gentle heart,
A simple thing called life;
A simple dream to be made possible,
A gentle reminder of a majestic painting,
Painted the Master's hands,
A wonder of wonders,
A love between a man and a woman;
Oh what a sit to behold,
Thank You, Lord!

AND THE DARKNESS COMES

Out of nowhere it came;
From nowhere it came,
Darkness encompasses my heart,
Darkness encompasses my soul,
Age 33, temptation peaks at heights unknown,
Age 33, nowhere to go darkness dwells,
Down on my knees I confess to the Lord,
My sins, my wrongs, I ask for forgiveness
A memory peaks through the darkness;
At age six, I ask Jesus into my life,
A revival with angels in waiting to protect me;
From the demons below,
An arrow of light shoots through the darkness,
Of my soul,
An arrow strong with conviction strikes my heart;
An arrow full in faith,
An arrow deep with hope,
An arrow bonded with love,
On my knees a stirring from within breaks through the darkness
At age 33, I hear a whisper within my heart,
The whisper say," You are still my child,
And you're forgiven of your sins."
Out with the old in with the new,
At age 33, a reminder that is gentle and true;
The Lord is always there no matter how far I may stray.
The Lord welcomes me home with open arms;
A gentle reminder I am His miracle,
For I could not overcome the darkness without;
The Lord's guidance and wisdom,
For out of the darkness comes an arrow of light,
To warm my heart and my soul;
Thank You, Lord, for always being their for me

THE WIND A GENTLE REMINDER

A strong wind blows within my heart;
A wind blowing with faith encompasses my soul,
A wind blowing with hope strong and true,
A wind blowing with unlimited love,
Encompasses my heart with conviction;
Conviction that warms my soul,
A friend with an invisible touch;
Touch gentle and true,
For the wind blows to and fro,
A gentle reminder of a friend of mine,
A friend named Jesus,
A friend ready to counsel me,
A friend in faith, hope, and love

A BLESSED MORNING TO BE

Upon one morning,
I saw a beautiful light,
To me it was a sight to adore;
A sight to rejoice,
My guardian angel comes to me;
In the morning sunrise, my angel comes knocking at my door.
Upon opening my door,
My angel asks to come in,
I pulled up a chair, and we sat and talked.
My angel told me to have faith,
My angel told me to have hope,
My angel told me to have love,
In the midst of talking, my angel gets quiet.
My angel said with a smile,
"I have come to take you home."
A moment of confusion;
Then I turned to see my body still in my bed.
Sadness overcomes me,
Then a peace and joy comes to my heart.
I took my angel's out stretched hand,
Then it was over a book ended;
But a majestic new chapter started, upon my death
Thank You, Lord!

A GUARDIAN ANGEL STEADY AND TRUE

Upon the clouds high above me;
Stands tall an angel,
Of noble spirit and heart,
That is a resolute protector,
A faith within shines forth;
A hope within shines bright,
A love within shines outward to all,
Steady and true my guardian angel;
Waits my cries of fear and doubt,
Cries of help in time of need,
There steady and true with conviction;
My guardian angel comes to my need,
Thank You Lord!

A BLESSED MORNING

I see a most wondrous sight;
Through the morning fog,
I see a marvelous sight;
Colors of creation I see,
Read of love,
Yellow of hope,
Blue of faith,
Other colors dance of joy;
Everlasting friendship indeed,
One sight revealed in the Lord,
An everlasting foundation forevermore;
A marriage made in love, faith, and hope
A promised revealed through the Lord's creation.

SHE HAD BROWN EYES OF PASSION

I looked deep into her eyes;
A depth unknown in those eyes she had,
Deep with tenderness I saw in those eyes;
Deep with love I saw in those eyes,
Deep with faith I saw in those eyes,
Deep with hope I was in those eyes,
Dreams to be kindled between a man and a woman;
Fires within burns bright and true,
As two hearts beat in unity;
A chapter begins anew in two lives,

THE FOLLY OF WORDS SAID IN ANGER

The folly of being human;
She is a demon of fire;
She has fine gold locks of hair,
That falls down upon her shoulders,
Blue eyes that spit fire;
She snares the unsuspecting male,
Promises of faith,
Promises of hope,
Promises of love,
Empty lies she promises;
Dust to dust,
Promises are blown to the wind;
Wind that comes from nowhere,
Wind that leaves nothing but an empty heart;
Heart black as the night sky,

Miracles Of The Heart

Romans 12: 15-17(NKJV)
"Rejoice with those who rejoice, and weep with those who weep.
Be of the same mind toward one another. Do not set your mind
on high things, but associate with the humble. Do not be wise
in your own opinion. Repay no one evil for evil.
Have regard of good things in the sight of all men.

ROMANS 12: 1, 2(NKJV)
"I beseech you therefore, brethren, by the mercies of God,
that you present your bodies a living sacrifice, holy,
acceptable to God, which is your reasonable service.
And do not be conformed to this world, but be transformed
by the renewing of your mind, that you may prove what
is that good and acceptable and perfect will of God"

PAST THE PAIN
TO THE GRACE OF THE LORD

Matthew 6:34 (NKJV) "Therefore do not worry about tomorrow, for tomorrow will worry, about its own thing. Sufficient for the day is its own trouble."

Hello, my name is Paul Smith, I seek rest but I am harsh and very judgmental of myself. I have tried through the years to seek forgiveness from the Lord, but I now know it is too late for me. It is because the years of running from something that escapes explanation. I came to the party to seek rest; so now I am willing to give in, for I can run no farther from what the Lord has planned for my life.

I sit in a chair in a crowded room of people I have long since forgotten their names. I blend into the shadows as I have done the years before. I look across the room, and I recognize nobody at this party. My eyes gently grow heavy as I nod off to sleep, and I very quietly slip into dreams of comfort and peace. A gentle wind seems to arouse my senses as I sleep here in this chair. A whisper softly and gently echoes in my head.

Whisper says, "Paul, please wake up, please, Paul."

I stir but sleep is such a comfort I do not want to wake up. The dreams are too peaceful to wake from them.

A hand is gently placed on my shoulder to gently shake me awake. Again, I hear the whisper say something to me as I try shaking the dust of the sandman from my head and eyes.

Whisper says, "Paul, are you awake? Paul, Paul."

My eyes start to adjust to the light as the cobwebs start to fall from my head. The hand is still on my shoulder as my head lifts, and eyes open to see a sight that is before me. The face is familiar, but yet I am unable to place the face of the woman; which is standing before me.

Paul asks, "Are you an angel?"

Woman replies, "No, silly, I am not an angel, my name is Jennifer."

Paul asks, "But how can one be so beautiful, and not be an angel?"

Jennifer blushes a bit but inhales then exhales a breathe before she replied to Paul's question. For it surprised her that even after all these years the feelings for Paul were still strong and true within her. Even though, seeing Paul was a surprise at the party. Paul had been the only man to treat her with honor and respect. Paul treated her as if each day would be the last, and she failed to understand that when they had first meet those years ago. Until she had read one of the many Bible verses that was dear to Paul's heart. The one that came to Jennifer's mind was 1 Samuel 16:7. Before replying to Paul's question, Jennifer quietly spoke this verse to herself to find the strength and courage to talk to Paul after all these years.

Jennifer whispered, **"But the Lord said to Samuel, "Do not look at his appearance or his physical stature, because I have refused him, for the lord does not see as man sees, for man looks at the outward appearance, but the Lord looks at the heart. 1 Samuel 16:7."(NKJV)**

Jennifer replies, "The only beauty I see is of the Lord Jesus Christ."

Then a memory, of the past, starts to push through the fog as I sit and stare at the young woman before me. I remember a small four year-old girl my mom baby sat when I was a young boy. The first time my mom took care of, a baby boy and his sister; both were a sight to see as they explored their new environment. I was sitting on the floor. Me, I was sitting on the floor with my back to the couch, and sitting on the floor with my legs in a v position. The little girl of four with brown hair and brown eyes finally is curious of the human being on the floor in the living room. She crawls over one leg of the boy, with brown hair and blue eye, sitting on the floor. She sits between the boy's legs for awhile. They just sit there until the little girl loses interest and gets up to play. What amazes the boy is she came to sit by him of her own free will. He did nothing to get her attention because deep down he knew he was not worthy of such attention from a little girl. The memory fades as it dawns upon Paul who he sees before him.

Paul is thirty years-old now with gray hairs that match the life he has lived, and the personal hell he lives each day of his life. Each movement of his bones brings pain to his body. A thought occurs to Paul, I am not worthy to behold such a beautiful sight.

Paul sees a woman of twenty-five years that stands, at 5'11, before him. She is petite with an athletic build that defines her beauty. The purple evening dress she wears shows off her brown eyes that hold a passion deep and dear. Her eyes also sparkle of life, and she has long curly brown hair that falls down upon her shoulders.

Paul says, "Jennifer?!"

Jennifer answers, "Yes Paul."

Jennifer sees a handsome man of thirty standing before her. He is athletic built and stands straight and true that defines the man before her. He has short wavy brown hair with blue eyes that speak of the hurts and disappointments of the past heartaches.

Paul stands to look at a piece of his past; which he had long forgotten. Their hands intertwine as a signal of recognition that what they both see is real and not a dream. A soft melody of music plays as they stand there talking and taking in each other.

Paul asks, "Jennifer would you like to dance?"

Jennifer answers, "Yes I would like that very much."

The music is soft and slow for each other to talk, and enjoy one another's company. As arms intertwine each other dance to the soft music. Paul stares up into Jennifer's soft brown eyes to see the gentleness and softness in her eyes, but Paul also sees the hurts and the pains of the years past. He pulls her closer to comfort her as the music plays. They just dance to the music not knowing what to say to each other.

A tear stars down Jennifer's cheek.

Jennifer whispers softly, "I have found you my sweet prince."

Paul looks up at her not knowing what to say. They lock eyes and they know they don't want this moment in time to end. Their hearts merged into one complete heart beating to one steady beat upon eye contact. The music begins to fade and the dancing stops, but neither one wants to release one another from their embracing one another. As they continue looking into each others eyes.

Before this goes further Paul breaks contact with Jennifer and lets her go. Their hearts start beating separate beats again. Paul and Jennifer just stand there not knowing what to say one another. It just seems impossible to Paul, but deep within his heart he knows it is to be. The Lord has made impossibility into a possibility in Paul's life.

Paul speaks, "Jennifer I am an old man who is used up. I have seen too much pain, and it seems when I get close to someone something bad always happens to them. I will forever cherish this moment I thank you."

Jennifer starts to speak, but Paul stops her by softly putting his finger on her lips.

Paul speaks, "Jennifer if you must remember me then remember that you have met a real life Charlie Brown."

Paul starts to walk away, but Jennifer grabs his arm before he gets to far from her.

Jennifer speaks, "It is the Lord that has lead me to you. Paul you are the Lord's creation. I see beyond your pain, and love the man who stands before me. While we danced you comforted me, and you saw past the pain in me. Don't run from the Lord, but embrace what the Lord has given you."

Paul stands not knowing what to say to Jennifer. Then his walls of defense start to crumble. He turns to face Jennifer for he can not believe the wisdom she has spoken to him. Then something wet starts its journey down his cheek and Paul sees Jennifer that she is doing the same thing.

Jennifer whispers, "My prince."

Paul whispers, "My princess."

The man and woman embrace one another as if they have found their missing puzzle pieces to their lives. Their two hearts become one whole heart beating to one steady beat beating with faith, hope, and love given by the Lord upon this most precious union of man and woman. A moment in time is all it takes, when we allow the Lord to bring mercy and grace into our lives to replace our fears and doubts.

ECCLESAISTES 3:1-22(niv)

ECC 3:1 There is a time for everything,
and a season for every activity under heaven:
ECC 3:2 a time to be born and a time to die,
a time to plant and a time to uproot,
ECC 3:3 a time to kill and a time to heal,
a time to tear down and a time to build,
ECC 3:4 a time to weep and a time to laugh,
a time to mourn and a time to dance,
ECC 3:5 a time to scatter stones and a time to gather them,
a time to embrace and a time to refrain,
ECC 3:6 a time to search and a time to give up,
a time to keep and a time to throw away,
ECC 3:7 a time to tear and a time to mend,
a time to be silent and a time to speak,
ECC 3:8 a time to love and a time to hate,
a time for war and a time for peace.
ECC 3:9 What does the worker gain from his toil? 10 I have seen the burden God has laid on men. 11 He has made everything beautiful in its time. He has also set eternity in the hearts of men; yet they cannot fathom what God has done from beginning to end. 12 I know that there is nothing better for men than to be happy and do good while they live. 13 That everyone may eat and drink, and find satisfaction in all his toil--this is the gift of God. 14 I know that everything God does will endure forever; nothing can be added to it and nothing taken from it. God does it so that men will revere him.
CC 3:15 Whatever is has already been,
and what will be has been before;
and God will call the past to account.n
ECC 3:16 And I saw something else under the sun:
In the place of judgment--wickedness was there,
in the place of justice--wickedness was there.
ECC 3:17 I thought in my heart,
"God will bring to judgment

both the righteous and the wicked,
for there will be a time for every activity,
a time for every deed."
ECC 3:18 I also thought, "As for men, God tests them so that they may see that they are like the animals. 19 Man's fate is like that of the animals; the same fate awaits them both: As one dies, so dies the other. All have the same breathn; man has no advantage over the animal. Everything is meaningless. 20 All go to the same place; all come from dust, and to dust all return. 21 Who knows if the spirit of man rises upward and if the spirit of the animaln goes down into the earth?"

ECC 3:22 So I saw that there is nothing better for a man than to enjoy his work, because that is his lot. For who can bring him to see what will happen after him?

A COMET'S STORY OF FAITH, HOPE, AND LOVE
(fiction)

**"AND NOW ABIDE FAITH, HOPE, AND LOVE, THESE THREE, BUT THE GREATEST OF THESE IS LOVE."
1CORINTHINANS 13:13 (NKJV)**

Once, in the deepest reaches of space, there were two comets that cherished each others company. The more time they spent together the brighter the two comets got, and their tails stretched bright and strong. Then one day in their travels they come upon a bright colorful planet that emitted strange energy and sound. The boy comet wanted to explore the planet, but the girl comet wanted to continue to explore space and the stars in it. The boy comet quickly came to a decision. He turned toward the planet and headed straight toward the colorful planet to explore. The gravity of the planet was strong and pulled the boy comet quickly into the planet's atmosphere. Before he could stop he made a big splash in what he thought was called water.

Up above in the vastness of space the girl comet continued along her adventure of exploring space and stars among it. A strange quietness engulfed her, and she felt as though she had lost something dear to her heart. She gathered speed as she headed away from the planet in which the boy comet had took off to explore. What was different was her brightness and tail began to fade as she traveled the stars. Still a bright star just loneliness engulfed her as she headed away from the planet that took the boy comet. Now she wished upon a bright shooting stare that passed by her that in faith, hope, and love she would meet him again.

When the boy comet came to a stop upon the strange planet something had changed. He was no longer a bright shining star. He was a human with a real body that was soaking wet, and covered by wet and strange looking blue garments that he did not recognize. He was floating in blue water. Fear started to over take him, but the thought of the girl comet seemed to beat back the fear. A faith, hope, and love seemed to encompass his heart and soul. An assurance deep within his heart he would see the girl comet again. Upon this thought he rose from the blue water and started to walk upon the water. Each wave and ripple tickled his feet, but soon adjusted to the new feeling. So his adventure upon this planet began.

He looked fare and wide on the planet for a kindred spirit and found none. So he continued walking upon the planet for he could no longer fly. Though he yearned for flight he could not do this one simple action while on the planet. So he continued walking to and fro upon the waters of the planet searching, for a place of rest; for he was weary of his time spent on this planet.

Then one day, just as the fog was lifting he came upon an island in the blue waters he traveled upon. The closer he came to the island he saw the beauty of the island seemed to call to him. As he reached the shore weariness started to overtake him. He stepped on to the sandy shore, and a message appeared in front of him.

HE WHO HAS FAITH WILL BE ABLE TO WALK UPON THE SANDS OF TIME. BEWARE OF YE OF LITTLE FAITH FOR SURELY YOU WILL DIE.

This message perplexed him, but at the same time the message made sense. He began to walk upon the sands of the island, but to his surprise he began to sink in the sand on the shore. He struggled, but the more he struggled the quicker he sank in the sand. Then he remembered the girl comet, and the faith he would meet her again; and when he thought of this wonderful reunion he began to rise from the sand onto solid ground. He began his exploration of the island. In the distance, he saw a huge mountain rise out of the middle of the island; so he decided to head in a straight path for the mountain. By mid day he reached the beautiful and colorful jungle area of the island. To his surprise he found a clear path to walk upon.

Again, another message appeared before him before he could step on to the path.

YE FULL OF HOPE SHALL PASS THROUGH THE JUNGLE OF FEAR UNSCATHED. YE WHO DOUBT YE SHALL PERISH.

This time he thought before he moved. He had faith he would see her again, and he had hope that the day would come soon to be reunited with her. When he began to walk the path he noticed that an energy he had not felt in a while returning to him. He walked with a faith and a hope as a man who was about to accomplish a great task set before him. He did not see or hear anything except a wind that was rustling the leaves on the trees. Soon he came upon the foot of the mountain, and it was a most beautiful sight to take in and to ponder upon.

Then out of nowhere a piece of fruit appeared and a message appeared just above the piece of fruit.

HE WHO EATS THIS FRUIT WILL BE FILLED. A CLIMB IN LOVE WILL ACCOMPLISH A GREAT TASK AT HAND. IN THE END, A GREAT MIRALE IS DONE UPOON THE END OF ONE'S QUEST.

He reached out for the piece of fruit and to his amazement it was real. He ate in peace, and as he ate strength returned to him. Then all of the sudden he began to glow a bright blue, and as soon as it happened it stopped. He decided to climb the mountain with the faith, hope, and love in his heart. He was excited as if the end of his quest was near an end.

The climb was hard for the footing and the places to grip were hard to find on the mountain. But as he got the feel of the mountain a rhythm began to go through his head which made the climb go quickly on him. He was at the top of the mountain before he knew it.

Night had fallen so as soon as he was able to view it he saw the wide open ocean; which glowed in the moonlit night. A gentle breeze blew across the area in which he stood. Then he chose to sit and stare up at the clear night sky for the stars twinkled bright and strong. The more he stared at the stars the brighter the blue he glowed.

Up in space, the girl comet came shooting through the stars. A light caught her eye as she came upon a planet where a bright blue light pulsed of life. The pulse of life in the blue light felt familiar to her. Could it be? This was not possible, but at the same time deep within her heart it was possible. Her journey had led her back to the planet where she and the boy comet had separated so long ago. With the speed of the faith, hope, and love she had in her heart she headed toward the blue light. As she came closer to the planet the gravity pull of the planet was strong upon her. A change in her started to take place. The loneliness that had engulfed her seemed to leave her. She saw a small island in the midst of a great ocean of water. For, it was night time so the island was engulfed in blackness except for the moon and a bright blue light. As she came nearer to the island a change seem to take place in her. A peace in which she longed forgotten came over her. Also at this moment she began to glow a bright red. She noticed she was wearing a bright red garment worn by humans.

The island came upon her quickly so she made a loud crash as she came upon the mountain at the center of the island drifting in the ocean.

The boy comet stood up as he heard the crash. He saw a place where the dirt had been unearthed. A bright red glow seemed to catch his eye as if he could not believe his eyes that the red glow was the girl comet as he stared at the beautiful red glow.

She pushed herself up to her feet and brushed the dirt off her garments and body. Then she sensed that a pair of blue eyes was staring at her. She looked over to where she sensed the presence. She saw a most joyous sight before her eyes. Before her stood the boy comet, but he no longer was the boy comet she knew once upon a time. He had grown into an adult man comet. A most beautiful sight; of bright blue garments that shimmered in the moonlit night.

The boy comet saw a majestic bright red figure standing before him. His heart skipped a beat when he saw not a girl, but an adult woman comet. In beautiful red garments that shimmered in the moonlit night.

When their eyes meet the beating of their hearts became one steady beat instead of two separate beating hearts. Their hearts seemed to join in together upon looking at one another. At first, all the two comets could do was look at one another in amazement. Then they took a step forward at the same time. First it was slow and steady walk, and then each step became a little quicker until they started running toward one another. In a brief moment, when the man comet and woman comet embraced one another a magical change took place among the man and the woman. A most sacred reunion was made only by the Master's hands could this have been made. Time seemed to slow down at the moment of their embrace. The colors of red and blue seemed to merge into a majestic royal purple bright as the sun in the morning... A pause took place as they released one another they changed back to the colors red and blue and their hearts began beating separately from one another.

The man spoke first to the beautiful woman standing before him.

Man said, "My beloved, I have found my kindred spirit for I have searched far and wide on the planet. I have found none that compared to your beauty and spirit. For in faith, hope, and love I have found you. My precious love, will you be mine forever and ever for all eternity?"

For a moment she was breathless, and then she inhaled and exhaled slowly to gather her thoughts. Then she began to speak to the handsome man that stood before her.

Woman said, "My beloved, I have traveled the stars far and wide searching, yet I could not find anyone that was as sweet and as pure as you. You my love are my kindred spirit. Yes, I will be yours forever and ever for all eternity. For in faith, hope, and love we have found one another."

At that moment, they embraced one another a change took place in both of them. A majestic royal purple seemed to come to be as the man and woman embraced one another. Their hearts merged into one heart beating as one whole heart. A shimmer of purple light began to glow bright and strong in them and outside of them.

Upon completion of the change, they began to rise steadily into the air heading toward the stars in the night sky. As their speed increased the stars and space called out to them as they broke free of the planet's gravity.

A union most special created by the Master's hands; a man to a woman, a union made in faith, hope, and love under the Lord's watchful eyes. So if you are ever star gazing at night and you see a purple light streak across the night sky you know it is the male and female comet of a union made for eternity. Their showing others that a bond of faith, hope, and love cannot be broken, but is forever edged into time to remain unbroken when we believe in one another.

THE BATTLE AT SUNSET

"I am the Alpha and the Omega, the Beginning and the End, says the Lord, who is and who was and who is to come, the Almighty." Revelation 1:8(nkjv)

"You are worthy, O Lord, to receive glory and honor and power; for You created all things, and by Your will they exist and were created." Revelation 4:11 (nkjv)

A magnificent sight takes place at a day's end as time stands still. At this moment in time, a battle starts between the glowing light and the bleak darkness. Each color, sound, and smell represents a soldier in battle against the enemy. The senses awake to the ongoing war suspended in time. The cry of war bells sound the rising and setting of each day.

Looking at the majestic sunset reminds me of the medieval battles of good and evil. Each color of the sunset has its duty during the battle to stay alive. The leader of the battle is fire red, with his golden sword leading the charges. His soldier, flaming orange, stands at his side clashing swords together against the swift storm of darkness. Red and orange battle, while other colors are more inert in their fight. Bright pink just flirts with dark saying, "I will do a favor for the dark as long as the dark goes away." The pink battles with his wits as darkness overpowers him making him lose his mind game. Lemon yellow, with his dancing shoes, dances with dark time and again trying to tire dark out. But the dark does not give in. The violet purple rages, with an iron fist, alongside red and orange as the swords and fists fly among enemies making sparks of hatred. When the battle ends the colors say, 'Wait until next time." It is time to say retreat once more. The wounded soldiers regroup as they fade into the background with streaks of disgust and burning hurts. They say, "We will meet again!"

The bleak darkness shouts with glee at another victory, as the musty smell of grass and the wet dew settles on the cold ground. The gray smoke is settling, as this was a bloody battle between these two forces. For no matter how much blood was shed, the black shadows, and creeping creatures of the dark are happy of their victory. The musicians of the bleak darkness strike up their annoying victory music along with other sounds of the night. The pesky animals of the shadows sing along with the music in time of happy celebration. The shadows shout with glee and dance around with a mischievous smile showing their boasting, but their boasting will not last for long. The war cries of the light are heard in the background. For the dark knows the dark will fade into the background with burning wounds of defeat and disgust.

The battle at the transition of day or night is a magnificent sight to see. This is a war between light and dark, in which the battle is an endless one. Neither side really wins. They just add a minor victory to there score cards. Their wounds heal quickly as each new day starts, as they begin another wasted effort on fighting. Neither of the two forces really triumphs just one continuous chain reaction of Mother Nature that never stops.

ABOUT THE AUTHOR

JOURNEY OF THE HEART CONTINUES ONA TRUE MIRACLE STORY
(nonfiction)

FOR WE WALK BY FAITH, NOT BY SIGHT," 2CORINTIANASNS 5:7(NKJV)

Hello, my name is William Garrett Woodard age 33 single, Christian male who is amazed at how the Lord works His miracles and blessings each day we wake up to in our lives. What is so breathe taking to know is that the Lord has added to my testimony instead of taking away like most Christians make the mistake in believing in Jesus. In faith, hope, and love the Lord has shown me that sometimes living just one day at a time is a testimony of the Lord's love has for each and every one of us. My story is not yet finished, but is filled with the Lord and His blessings. It is hard to know where to begin and end my story. So let us begin at the crucial point in where we first meet Jesus and that is when we accepted Jesus Christ as our Savior.

    Honestly, I do not know how to start this story because each time I try to write my testimony of what the Lord has done in my life I start to cry. I am amazed how the Lord loves and protects His children every step they take, and guiding them in life whether or not we know it. The time in my life I am about to tell about is about faith, hope, love, life, and death. For me death came for me, but the

Lord gave me life in one of my darkest of hours. The Lord showed me what it is meant to have family that cares for me, and loves me beyond my imperfections and how He works His miracles right before our eyes.

The year is 1978, and I am six years-old and still a growing boy. Two big events are about to change my life forever, and years later I only then realize the importance of these events in my life. The first big and most important event was me being saved at a revival at six years of age. Giving your life to Jesus know matter the time in your life will always be imprinted upon your heart as it has been mine. I still use this point in my life to see where I have been, and to see where the Lord is taking me upon this journey called life. Well, on with the story, I hope you are able to see the miracle of Jesus and His awesome love He has for His children.

I was at a revival with my family at Wildwood Baptist Church Joplin, MO. It was hot that summer evening, and the revival was held out side on the church's grounds. The meeting place was made of wood poles, metal chairs, and a roof made of leaves and branches. People were fanning with some sort of flyer because it was hot that evening. Then the invitation was given, and I turned to my parents sitting next to me I would like to go up and ask Jesus into my heart. I was excited and hardly could contain my excitement. My parents, Ron and Linda Woodard, asked me to make sure I knew what I was doing. They finally said okay and took me up to the pastor and he asked me the questions and I accepted Jesus as my savior and presented to the people for baptism. A couple of Sundays later I was baptized along with my older brother, Ronald Gail Woodard II, as a representation of washing away the old me and putting on the new me. I would not realize the significance of this one action and decision until much later in life. It is a gentle reminder of when I started my walk with Jesus, and that we all must have child like faith to know the Lord.

The second big event that occurred in my life that was to shake my foundation and forever reshape my world and my family. This happened about four months after I had given my life to Jesus. Being young when you accept Jesus at the time you don't realize how much the Lord is watching over until later in life, and you let the fears and doubts creep into your life. This still continues in my life, and I am still learning about the Lord and His all encompassing love He has for all of us. I do hope you are able to see the faith, hope, and love the Lord has for us. So on with story that seemed to define who I am before I knew the purpose of what the Lord had for me in life.

On December 22, 1978, I, William G. Woodard, and my family were in a car wreck on 32nd Street. Joplin, MO. We were struck from behind by a drunk driver going 55mph in a 40mph speed zone. What I am about to tell of the events that transpired has been told to me by my parents. For I have no memory of the event in my life so let us continue on with the story.

The day was like no other winter day two brothers fighting over who gets to sit behind mom. I being the youngest got his way, and now until the day I die I am glad I got to sit behind mom. When the drunk driver hit our vehicle it forever changed four lives. My dad, Ron Woodard, suffered a severe whiplash, my older brother, Ronald G. Woodard II, received a bruised back and rug burn. My mom, Linda Woodard, received broken ribs and collar bone. Me, I did not escape injury and what happened to me was not a small injury. This is what is amazing about the Lord was he was right there all the time I learned to survivor one day at time.

I, William, did not come out of the car wreck as lucky as did my family. I received a severe head injury which put me in to coma for 18 days. The doctors that operated on me and saw me after surgery only gave me a 50/50 chance of living, and the odds were that when I awoke from coma I would be mentally disabled for the rest of my life. When I awoke from coma I had lost my memory, motor skills, verbal skills, and other skills. I had to relearn the basic of skills and with my parents encouraging and instilling a faith, hope, and love. I relearned to talk even though it took me four years. I eventually relearned everything I had lost even though it was hard relearning everything. From the head injury also I am half-blind, which means an optic nerve was severed during my head injury and this controls the left vision in both my eyes. So I am unable to see people coming up on my left side. I learned to compensate for what I had lost in the car wreck, and to adapt to different situations that came up in my life. I almost had a steel plate put in my head if my soft spot did not hardened up; which it did harden. I live with an indention on my skull to this day. I also had steel staples put in my head to hold my skull together after surgery and a scar on my skull. Each time I recall the story my parents told me I was a miracle and I got the nickname the miracle kid. I know now it was an act of Jesus' love for me and my life. So I may testify of His love, miracles and blessings each day I live and breathe. The Lord put my back together better than I was before the car wreck. I would not take it back for anything because I am still living with my limitations the Lord gave me to overcome. One day at time in faith, hope, and love. Jesus taught me to survive through the love of family and friends.

Another event that was a direct result of the head injury would come six years later at age of twelve, but there would be warning signs of the change to come in my life. I would learn to lean upon the Lord even when He seems so far away. At the age of nine, I was having black out seizures in the classroom at school. I would just stop functioning and start staring into space. At the time they were small and did not require medication. I was okay until three years later at the age of twelve.

When I was twelve years-old I started to have full blown grandma seizures. This is where an electrical brain wave is going along its pathway and it hits a brick wall and bounces off and introducing to the body a totally different action than intended. I would fall down and start to shake uncontrollably and my eyes would roll back in my head and my speech and thought process would seem to go haywire. The danger was in the amount of time the seizure took because damage to my head could result, nothing, coma, death, but all that happened was a loss of memory and being extremely tired. Again, the Lord was there handling everything even though I did not know it. The Lord guided the doctor in diagnosing my problem and to the right medication to control my seizures. For over eighteen years, the Lord kept me seizure free through the medication and other solutions for my disabilities to help me cope with on a daily basis.

During the time I was twelve and now at the age of thirty-three I am awestruck by the miracles, blessings and how the Lord reveals His mysteries to us. My list of accomplishments could not have been done without the Lord being there in every part of my life.

Even when I turned a deaf ear the Lord would still be there guiding me through the dark times in my life.

After, completion of high school at Diamond High School Diamond, MO in May 1990. This was a big accomplishment for me because the doctors said I would be unable to learn past the sixth grade level of learning. This I believe was the start of things to come in my life and what the Lord has accomplished in my life. The Lord has made impossibilities into possibilities in my life. I would go on and earn two college degrees to add to my list of accomplishments. I earned an Associates of Arts in Elementary Education at Crowder College Neosho, MO. I graduated in May 1994 from Crowder College, but learned to write poetry and short stories while I was there and continue to do so. One of my college papers, The Battle at Sunset, was published by the Crowder Quill in 1992. This helped with my confidence and instilled a creative ability I had not realized I had before. I learned to communicate, verbal skills and other lessons at Crowder College. At this time, I had just been doodling with poetry and short stories never really taking an interest it was more of a hobby and to help with stress. The Lord had his hand in this all the time I was there and continues until this day.

Upon graduating Crowder College, I went to Missouri Southern State College, renamed MSSU, to complete my college education. I learned to stand firm in the values and morals the Lord have given to my parents to instill in me. Learned to lean upon the Lord; and He will get you through the tough times in life when fear and doubt want to overtake us. I had changed majors while I was at Southern. I started in Elementary Education, but ended up with a degree in General Studies with an emphasis in business. The degree I earned was a Bachelor's of General Studies upon completing the courses in December 1997. Another blessing the Lord had given to me to have to show how the Lord works in our lives and especially through caring and supportive parents and friends. Learned to read the Bible and apply the Lord's teachings to my life and situations that come my way on a daily basis

The tough times were yet to come in my life. I was hurt by friend's actions in church and left the church for a time, but I still continued reading scripture and the Bible on a daily basis during this dark time in my life. In November 1998, I was hired on at Target Joplin, MO to work flow which was unloading and stocking the shelves. But during my time at Target I learned to stand firm in my convictions, moral, and values the Lord has given to me; while I was at Target Joplin, MO. My time at Target would be from Nov. 1998-Oct. 2005.

I would accomplish some of my dreams in which seemed impossible was made possible by the Lord. In 2003, while recovering from elbow surgery I entered my poetry in a poetry contest on the Website www.poetry.com. They sent me forms to inform that my poem, Kindling of Dreams, had been chosen to be published in one of their poetry books. I could not believe this but had happened my poetry had been published. I thank the Lord for helping take a leap of faith and for making a small dream of mine come true. I continue to write poetry to this day I found out it is a great way to thank the Lord and to capture our thoughts and feelings on paper.

When the year 2004 had started, I had no idea of what the Lord had in store for me. I was still working at Target and still taking seizure medication in 2004. I took tegretol for seizure medication and was taking carbratol another form or tegretol ; which was quicker releasing. I went to the doctor regularly to make sure the medication was not harming my body. Well, I went to the doctor for my regular blood test and come to find out the results which were not good. My white blood count had been affected by the medication. The doctor sent me to a neurologist to get his opinion of the situation. He suggested to me to go off the medication and told me of the risks of going off the medication. I would lose my driver licenses if I had seizure within six months of going of the medication. Or I could try other medications. I chose to go off the medication after eighteen years of being on the medication, and remaining seizure free during this time. The doctor took me off the medication, and on April 29, 2004 was the day in which I went off the medication. I have been seizure free without medication for over a year now going on two. Oh, the doctor also told me during the trial period my first six months off the medication would tell if I would ever have a seizure again. It has made a difference in my behavior, verbal skills, motor skills, and other skills. It was as if I had been in a fog and the fog had been lifted from my eyes. I was relearning skills which had been buried by the medication and my memory was sharper than before. I thank the Lord for giving me the information I needed to make the right decision in this situation.

So much has happened in my life that I only can say that it is the Lord's doing not mine. At thirty-three years old, I am still amazed at how the Lord works in our lives. I still do not drink alcohol, do not do drugs, do not chew tobacco, and do not party. Even through our dark times He is still there. I have gone back to church and continue reading the Bible and applying the Lord's word to my life. Prayer has been really helpful and writing and memorizing scripture to have with me on a daily basis one that is written upon my heart is 1Corithians 13:13 and I try daily to apply to my life on a daily basis.

Going to Mission Arlington in Arlington, TX (June 11th-17th 2005) open my eyes to how the Lord is involved in our lives on a daily basis. The Lord takes care of us each day no matter the situation in our lives. I am jobless right now but I am confident the Lord will show me the right direction in finding work and where the Lord leads me to do His work and His instrument. I thank the Lord for Miss Tillie and the mission team at Mission Arlington Thank you for showing I can make a difference no matter how small it seems in my eyes, but in the Lord's eyes it is a huge accomplishment. I think Ecc. 3:1 *"There is a time for everything and a season for every activity under heaven;"* (*NIV*) sums up a little on how the Lord reveals Himself to us daily through our actions and decisions we make on a daily basis.

Thank you.
God Bless you.
Your friend in Christ,
William G. Woodard

Psalm 62(NIV)

For the director of music. For Jeduthun. A psalm of David.
PS 62:1 My soul finds rest in God alone;
my salvation comes from him.
PS 62:2 He alone is my rock and my salvation;
he is my fortress, I will never be shaken.
PS 62:3 How long will you assault a man?
Would all of you throw him down--
this leaning wall, this tottering fence?
PS 62:4 They fully intend to topple him
from his lofty place;
they take delight in lies.
With their mouths they bless,
but in their hearts they curse.
Selah
PS 62:5 Find rest, O my soul, in God alone;
my hope comes from him.
PS 62:6 He alone is my rock and my salvation;
he is my fortress, I will not be shaken.
PS 62:7 My salvation and my honor depend on Godn;
he is my mighty rock, my refuge.
PS 62:8 Trust in him at all times, O people;
pour out your hearts to him,
for God is our refuge.
Selah
PS 62:9 Lowborn men are but a breath,
the highborn are but a lie;
if weighed on a balance, they are nothing;
together they are only a breath.
PS 62:10 Do not trust in extortion
or take pride in stolen goods;
though your riches increase,
do not set your heart on them.
PS 62:11 One thing God has spoken,

two things have I heard:
that you, O God, are strong,
PS 62:12 and that you, O Lord, are loving.
Surely you will reward each person
according to what he has done.

A NOTE FROM THE AUTHOR:

We all go through times in our lives that seem to be bleak and dismal on a daily basis. Writing poetry is a form of communicating what is on our hearts to the Lord. Even I go through situations that tempt me to do wrong in the eyes of the Lord (**1Peter 2:11**). Some things are best taken to the Lord in prayer and praise in our quiet times with the Lord. King David and King Solomon knew this in their lives. ***For we all sin and fall short of the Glory of the Lord (Romans 3:23)***. When we confess our sin to the Lord we are released of the burdens and given a clean slate on a daily basis ***(1Peter 5:7)***. We must hold one another accountable that we do not repeat the same mistakes each day. We must each day strive to read the Bible, pray, and be more Christ-like in every area of our lives each day we awake to on a daily basis. Me, I have found that each day is a new experience and the Lord is always waiting, ready, and willing to give His all to us. The Lord does reveal to us daily blessings, miracles, and mysteries that we see daily. So take one day a time seek the Lord out daily and the Lord will be there every step of the way. Make sure we are reading God's Word and applying what the Lord's word says to our hearts.

The Bible holds what is right and wrong, good and evil, morals and values we are to use as a measuring stick as we face daily temptations in all situations in our lives.

I Thank you, God Bless You, Sincerely, William G. Woodard

A Note of Thanks,

To my family who encouraged me on a daily basis to continue my writing poetry and short stories. My parents, Ron and Linda Woodard who are my sounding board and are true friends to talk to when I am down about life. My big brother, Ronald G. Woodard II, and his family. For, being there for me and encouraging me toward my goals. To the church family which has grown in these past years. Thank you First Baptist Church Diamond, MO and Northside Baptist Church Neosho, MO and Wild Wood Baptist Church Joplin, MO. Thank you goes to the Mission Team at Arlington, TX (JOHN3: 16) who showed me how the Lord works His blessings and miracles everyday of our lives. To Xulon Press and their people for taking a chance on me in getting my poetry and short stories published. Thank you all who shared a part of this journey with me in getting me dreams to become reality for me. Thank you and God Bless You. But most important the credit goes to the Lord and His Son Jesus Christ for being that steady rock in my life every step I take on a daily basis is a blessing and miracle from the Lord.

PSALM 1:1-6(NKJV)
   "**Blessed is the man who walks not in the counsel of the ungodly, not stands in the path of sinners, nor sits in the seat of the scornful; but his delight is in the law of the Lord, and in His law he meditates day and night. He shall be like a tree planted by the rivers of water that brings forth its fruit in its season, whose leaf also shall not wither; and what ever he does shall prosper. The ungodly are not so, but are like the chaff which the wind drives away. Therefore the ungodly shall not stand in the judgment, not sinners in the congregation f the righteous. For the Lord know the way of the righteous, but the way of the ungodly shall perish.**"

BIBILIOGRAPHY

God's Promises Bible New King James Version Bible, Thomas Nelson Bibles, 2003

Zordervan NIV Bible Library, version 2.5, 189-1997, The Zordervan Corporation

Printed in the United States
48080LVS00007B/67-165